A Student Guide to Chaucer's Middle English

A Student Guide to Chaucer's Middle English

Peter G. Beidler

coffeetownpress
Seattle, Washington

This book was set in Arial, Charis SIL, and Old English Text MT fonts by Marion Frack Egge.

Copyright © 2011 by Coffeetown Press, Seattle, Washington.

Contact: info@coffeetownpress.com

All rights reserved. With the exception of the exercises on pp. 50–55, no part of this book may be reproduced or transmitted in any form or by any means, electronic or mechanical, including photocopying, recording, or any information storage and retrieval system, without permission in writing from the publisher.

Cataloging-in-Publication Data

Peter G. Beidler
A Student Guide to Chaucer's Middle English / Peter G. Beidler
ISBN 978–1–60381–102–6

1. Chaucer's language. 2. Middle English. 3. Pronouncing Middle English. 4. Word List. 5. Canterbury Tales. 6. Geoffrey Chaucer (d. 1400). 7. Exercises.

Cover image: Ellesmere MS of Chaucer's *Canterbury Tales*
Cover design: Sabrina Sun

For Marion

**The opening lines of the *Canterbury Tales*
from the Ellesmere manuscript**

Courtesy the Huntington Library, San Marino, California

CONTENTS

ABOUT THE AUTHOR	viii
ACKNOWLEDGMENTS	ix
Chaucer Copied, Edited, Translated	1
The Ellesmere manuscript of the *Canterbury Tales*	1
A transcription of the first eighteen lines	3
An edited version of the first eighteen lines	4
A medley of modern English translations of the first four lines	7
Chaucer's Middle English	10
Old English roots	11
French loan words	13
Personal pronouns	14
Demonstrative pronouns	15
Verb forms	15
Adverbs and "-lich" forms	16
Double negatives and other small differences	16
Inconsistent spelling	17
Word List	19
Pronunciation and Phonetic Transcription of Chaucer's Middle English	25
Phonetic alphabet	26
Consonants	27
Vowels and diphthongs	31
More on vowels	38
Little words	39
The "schwa"	39
Other unstressed **e**'s	40
Iambic pentameter	40
Free tips	43
Practicing Transcription of Chaucer's Middle English	45
Transcribing a line	45
Start with the spelling, end with the pronouncing	47
Phonetic exercises	48

ABOUT THE AUTHOR

Peter G. Beidler is the Lucy G. Moses Professor of English, emeritus, at Lehigh University. He taught Chaucer at Lehigh for some forty years. In the course of that teaching he developed this guide to help his students grow familiar with Chaucerian Middle English—its origins, its development, its vocabulary, its sounds, its rhythms.

Beidler has published widely on Chaucer, including such books as *The Wife of Bath: Complete, Authoritative Text with Biographical and Historical Contexts, Critical History, and Essays from Five Contemporary Critical Perspectives* (1996), *Masculinities in Chaucer* (1998), *The Wife of Bath's Prologue and Tale: An Annotated Bibliography* (1998, with Elizabeth M. Biebel), *Geoffrey Chaucer's* Canterbury Tales (2006), and *Chaucer's Canterbury Comedies: Origins and Originality* (2011). He has also published on American literature (including contemporary Native American fiction), pedagogy, and composition.

He was named the National Professor of the Year in 1983 by CASE (Council for Advancement and Support of Education) and the Carnegie Foundation. Although he spent most of his career at Lehigh in Bethlehem, Pennsylvania, in 1987–88 he was a Fulbright professor at Sichuan University in Chengdu, China, and in 1995–96 was the Robert Foster Cherry Distinguished Teaching Professor at Baylor University in Waco, Texas.

The father of four children and grandfather to nine, he now lives with his wife Anne in Seattle, Washington.

ACKNOWLEDGMENTS

I thank the Huntington Library for permission to reproduce on the cover and on page x the opening lines of the Ellesmere manuscript of the *Canterbury Tales*.

Like most modern Chaucerians who are interested in the sounds of Chaucer's poetry, I owe a debt of gratitude to Helge Kökeritz for his ground-breaking *A Guide to Chaucer's Pronunciation* (University of Toronto Press, 1978). I found, however, that his twelve-page explanation was both too compact and too complex for undergraduate students encountering Middle English for the first time. I tried using his guide in my courses, but discovered that I was spending so much time filling in the gaps and unpacking his paragraphs that I decided to write my own more basic student guide, with background information on Chaucer's Middle English, a list of unfamiliar words that Chaucer used often, and my own more simplified, yet more fully developed explanation of what his verse sounded like.

I proudly express here my gratitude to two generations of Lehigh University students whose puzzled expressions, cautious questions, and pointed suggestions showed me how to make this guide better each time I taught my Chaucer course. But I specifically acknowledge here the help of one of those students. Marion Frack Egge was in one of my early courses. She later became my indispensable collaborator on a number of writing projects. She has helped me in many advisory, editorial, and technical ways with others. I gratefully dedicate this work to her.

Chaucer Copied, Edited, Translated

Chaucer died before he could finish the *Canterbury Tales*. Indeed he wrote fewer than a quarter of the 120 tales he at one time envisioned for the thirty pilgrims to tell to one another on their journey from London to Canterbury and back. The opening sequence, now known as the General Prologue, and most of the tales that he did finish, however, are so fine that most scholars call the *Canterbury Tales* Chaucer's masterpiece. So amazing is it that it has appeared in many editions and translations. The purpose of this chapter is to help you to understand how the modern editions and modern English translations reflect—or fail to reflect—what Chaucer actually wrote.

The Ellesmere manuscript of the *Canterbury Tales*

On the cover of this booklet is a reproduction of the opening eighteen lines of the General Prologue to the *Canterbury Tales* as they appear in the Ellesmere manuscript, the loveliest of the Chaucer manuscripts. A manuscript is by original definition enscripted manually. The Ellesmere is indeed a handwritten copy, but Chaucer did not make it. Indeed, none of the eighty-odd existing manuscripts of the *Canterbury Tales* is in Chaucer's handwriting.

Chaucer died in 1400. The Ellesmere manuscript is the work of a professional scribe who made the copy, on vellum (calfskin), probably for a wealthy patron, in the first decade after Chaucer's death. Recent research into medieval handwriting has shown that the scribe's name was Adam Pinkhurst, though we know little about him except his name.

The Ellesmere manuscript was purchased from its British owner in 1917 by the American railroad magnate Henry Huntington. It eventually became part of the Huntington Library in San Marino, California. Thanks to good luck and a carefully controlled environment, the vellum sheets are still almost as they were six centuries ago.

Each full manuscript page is almost twelve inches wide and sixteen inches high. A page typically contained almost fifty lines of careful quill-pen printing. Some pages have exquisite colored miniatures of individual Canterbury pilgrims.
A glance at the manuscript shows that Pinkhurst could make larger and smaller letters—we now call them uppercase and lowercase letters—and that he had access to skilled artists who could create large, ornate letters (see the elaborate opening "W" on the cover reproduction). A glance also shows that he ended each poetic line with a rhyming word. In these practices, he was typical of other Chaucerian scribes.

Pinkhurst, like other scribes of his time, did not use punctuation as we now know it. Indeed, most of the punctuation marks we now use had not yet been invented in Chaucer's time. There were no periods or commas, no apostrophes or quotation marks, no question marks or exclamation points, no colons or semicolons, no hyphens or dashes, no parentheses or brackets.

To be sure, there were slash marks (/), called "virgules," near the center of most lines, and an occasional raised dot, called a "punctus." The medieval scribe sometimes used the "paraph" sign (¶) at the start of a new narrative unit or speech, but there is no consistency in the placement of them. Indeed,

A transcription of the first eighteen lines 3

so far as we can tell, the use of all of these marks is scribal. That is, Chaucer may have used some of them in his own handwritten poems, but scribes like Adam Pinkhurst seem to have felt that punctuation was their own proper business and that they had license to put the virgules, the puncti, and the paraphs in or leave them out, according to their own judgment. Chaucer and his contemporaries, however, read and wrote Middle English without the benefit of what we now think of as punctuation.

Below are the opening eighteen lines of the General Prologue transcribed into modern letters and showing the virgules (which can be seen faintly on the cover image, more clearly on the black-and-white image on page x). These virgules seem not to have had much function, though they occasionally show up in these eighteen lines in places where we might consider a very brief pause or "caesura" in reading the line aloud. Occasionally a virgule appears where we might use a comma. Indeed, the virgule may in some sense be the ancestor of the modern comma. No puncti or paraphs appear in the opening eighteen lines.

A transcription of the first eighteen lines

Whan that Aprill with hise shoures soote
The droghte of march / hath perced to the roote
And bathed euery veyne / in swich licour
Of which vertu / engendred is the flour
Whan zephirus eek / with his sweete breeth   5
Inspired hath / in euery holt and heeth
The tendre croppes / and the yonge sonne
Hath in the Ram / his half cours yronne
And smale foweles / maken melodye
That slepen al the nyght / with open eye   10
So priketh hem nature in hir corages

Thanne longen folk / to goon on pilgrimages
And palmeres / for to seken straunge strondes
To ferne halwes / kowthe in sondry londes
And specially / fram euery shires ende   15
Of Engelond / to Caunterbury they wende
The hooly blisful martir for to seke
That hem hath holpen / whan þ^t they were seeke

Printed below is a modern-day edition of those first eighteen lines of the General Prologue. Here the editor has changed some letters to their modern equivalents (e.g., **u** to **v**), expanded contractions (e.g., þ^t to **that**), removed the virgules or slash marks, and regularized the spelling somewhat (e.g., in the first line, **hise** to **his**). He has also, of course, added modern punctuation like the comma, the period, the semicolon, and the parenthesis. In other passages, he used the question mark to indicate interrogation, the exclamation mark to indicate emphasis, quotation marks to indicate speech, and so on. This passage (like most of the Chaucerian passages quoted in this guide) is from the version in *The Riverside Chaucer*, ed. Larry D. Benson (Houghton Mifflin, 1987). This is the edition used by most scholars. The original editor of this version was Fred N. Robinson, whose editions of 1933 and 1957 earlier provided the basis for most scholarly research. We should be aware, then, that most critical judgments over the years have been based on edited versions of Chaucer designed for the ease of modern readers, rather than on the original manuscript readings themselves.

An edited version of the first eighteen lines

Whan that Aprill with his shoures soote
The droghte of March hath perced to the roote,
And bathed every veyne in swich licour

An edited version of the first eighteen lines 5

>Of which vertu engendred is the flour;
>Whan Zephirus eek with his sweete breeth   5
>Inspired hath in every holt and heeth
>The tendre croppes, and the yonge sonne
>Hath in the Ram his half cours yronne,
>And smale foweles maken melodye,
>That slepen al the nyght with open ye   10
>(So priketh hem nature in hir corages),
>Thanne longen folk to goon on pilgrimages,
>And palmeres for to seken straunge strondes,
>To ferne halwes, kowthe in sondry londes;
>And specially from every shires ende   15
>Of Engelond to Caunterbury they wende,
>The hooly blisful martir for to seke,
>That hem hath holpen whan that they were seeke.

There is much to say about this amazing passage. Note, for example, its when-then structure: "Whan" (line 1) . . . "Whan" (line 5) . . . "And [whan]" (line 9) . . . "Thanne" (line 12) . . . "whan" (line 18). And note the general progression upwards—from the physical to the spiritual, the inanimate to the animate, the plant world to the animal world to the human world—as Europe shakes off the cold of winter and embraces the warmth of spring. And note the progression from the general to the specific in human spiritual reactions to the earth's awakening: first it is generalized people (**folk**) longing to go on pilgrimage to undesignated foreign places (**straunge strondes**); then the people of England wanting to go to a specific shrine in their own land (**to Caunterbury**); and finally, in the next four lines, a specific person in a specific tavern in a specific place in London feels a specific springtime awakening call to travel to a the tomb of a specific English saint in a specific cathedral sixty miles to the southeast:

> Bifil that in that seson on a day,
> In Southwerk at the Tabard as I lay
> Redy to wenden on my pilgrymage
> To Caunterbury with ful devout corage. (19–22)

There are lots of modern English translations of the *Canterbury Tales*. Some of them are pretty good, some inaccurate, misleading, or just plain wrong. Even the pretty good ones, however, take us several steps away from what Chaucer actually wrote and several miles away from the way his spoken poetry actually sounded. I give below a medley of modern English "translations" of the first four lines of the General Prologue.

You will note that the translators into verse, in searching for rhymes and metrical regularity in their modern English renderings, have frequently had to insert words that Chaucer did not use. For example, most of the verse translators use "power" to rhyme with "flower," even though Chaucer did not use the word "power" in those lines. And where are the Chaucerian equivalents of Theodore Morrison's "bud and shoot," Rockwell Kent's "showers sweet with fruit," James J. Donahue's "March's feet," and Burton Raffel's flowers that "spring has always spread across these fields"?

Because the prose translators make no attempt to catch the rhythms or rhymes of Chaucer's verse, they tend to be more accurate than the verse ones, but even there we find problems. For example, Chaucer's **droghte** meant something more like "relative dryness" than "drought" in the modern parched-earth sense, and **licour** for Chaucer meant something more like "moisture" than "liquor" in the modern sense of an alcoholic beverage. And we should remember that while the **his** in the first line could indeed mean the gendered third-person pronoun "his," it also could mean the neutral "its." So we should be careful about assuming that Chaucer meant to anthropomorphize April into a male character, as most of the translators do by rendering **his** as "his" rather than "its." Besides, where in Chaucer's four lines do we find Peter Tuttle's suggestion that rain is "like virtue" or Peter Ackroyd's reference to humanity's rising up "in joy and expectation"?

Are we not better off with Chaucer's own words, forewarned that many of those words do not have their modern meaning? Are we not better off, if we want to know what Chaucer wrote, to read what Chaucer wrote?

To facilitate comparison with the Chaucerian original, I repeat Chaucer's own four lines here:

> **Whan that Aprill with his shoures soote**
> **The droghte of March hath perced to the roote,**
> **And bathed every veyne in swich licour**
> **Of which vertu engendred is the flour.**
> —Geoffrey Chaucer

A medley of modern English translations of the first four lines

Verse Translations

1. When in April the sweet showers fall
   And pierce the drought of March to the root, and all
   The veins are bathed in liquor of such power
   As brings about the engendering of the flower.
   —Nevill Coghill

2. When April with his showers hath pierced the drought
   Of March with sweetness to the very root,
   And flooded every vein with liquid power
   That of its strength engendereth the flower.
   —Frank Ernest Hill

3. As soon as April pierces to the root
   The drought of March, and bathes each bud and shoot
   Through every vein of sap with gentle showers
   From whose engendering liquor spring the flowers.
   —Theodore Morrison

4. When April with his showers sweet with fruit
   The drought of March has pierced unto the root
   And bathed each vein with liquor that has power
   To generate therein and sire the flower.
   —Rockwell Kent

5. When April with his showers fresh and sweet
   Has pierced the drouth that lies at March's feet,
   Bathing all roots and veins in liquid power
   Whose very aim and offspring is the flower.
   —James J. Donahue

6. When April's gentle rains have pierced the drought
   Of March right to the root, and bathed each sprout
   Through every vein with liquid of such power
   It brings forth the engendering of the flower.
   —Ronald L. Ecker

7. When April arrives, and with his sweetened shower
   Drenches dried-up roots, gives them a power
   To stir dead plants and sprout the living flowers
   That spring has always spread across these fields.
   —Burton Raffel

A medley of modern English translations of the first four lines

Prose Translations

8. When April with his sweet showers has pierced the drought of March to the root, and bathed every vein in such moisture as has power to bring forth the flower.
—A. Kent and Constance Hieatt

9. When April with his showers sweet the drought of March has pierced to the root and bathed every vein in such liquor, from whose virtue is engendered the flower.
—Vincent F. Hopper

10. When the sweet showers of April have pierced to the root the dryness of March, and bathed every vein in moisture whose quickening brings forth the flowers.
—John S. P. Tatlock and Percy MacKaye

11. When April with its gentle showers has pierced the March drought to the root and bathed every plant in the moisture which will hasten the flowering.
—Robert M. Lumiansky

12. When the sweet showers of April have pierced the dryness of March to its root and soaked every vein in moisture whose quickening force engenders the flower.
—David Wright

13. When April with his showers sweet the drought of March has pierced to the root, and rain, like virtue made those flowers grow.
—Peter Tuttle

14. When the soft sweet showers of April reach the roots of all things, refreshing the parched earth, nourishing every sapling and every seedling, then humankind rises up in joy and expectation.
—Peter Ackroyd

Chaucer's Middle English

It is not accurate to say, "I am reading Chaucer in Old English." Chaucer did not write, and did not even know how to read, Old English. Rather, he wrote in what is now called Middle English, though he would not have called it that. For him it was just the language he and his friends spoke and heard when they were not in church. That Chaucer and some of his countrymen wrote poetry and prose in English rather than in the more sophisticated French or the more learned Latin marks an amazing departure in the development of British literature.

It has become customary to divide the development of the English language into three overlapping periods. The Old English period ran from early times until around 1100, and includes the *Beowulf*-poet. The Middle English period ran from around 1100 to around 1500 and includes Chaucer. The modern English period runs from around 1500 to the present and includes Shakespeare, Milton, and later writers up to the present day.

Middle English is a hybrid language. Its base was the Old English language of the Anglo-Saxon people who were early immigrants into what are now the British Isles. Old English was a heavily Germanic language now almost unrecognizable to modern speakers of English, but was enriched and finally much altered by the French of the Norman conquerors who came across the English Channel in the eleventh century and began using their own language as the official language of the conquered nation.

Old English roots

Readers who are about to tackle Chaucer's Middle English might profit from knowing a couple of things about Old English. Old English marked grammatical function in large measure by what are called "inflections"—tags at the ends of certain words that showed whether the words were subjects or objects. In Old English, for example, there were several forms of the word we now know as "the," among them se (indicating the subject) and ðone (indicating the direct object). The letters ð (capitalized Ð) and þ (capitalized Þ), called an "eth" and a "thorn" respectively, are both roughly equivalent to the modern "th." In the simple Old English phrase, **Se mann æt ðone hund**, we would know that the man ate the dog because se tells us that **mann** is the subject or eater, while **ðone** indicates that **hund** is the object or one eaten. The word-order of the sentence was less important than the grammatical markers of the articles. If the sentence had read **Ðone hund æt se mann**, there would have been no change in meaning because the grammatical markers were the same. In Middle English, on the other hand, there was only the single form of the article "the." **The manne eet the hounde** meant something quite different from **The hounde eet the manne**, just as, in modern English "The man ate the dog" means something quite different from "The dog ate the man."

In part because the inflectional endings of Old English tended to grow weaker as time went by, Old English poetry tended to be alliterative, based on the sounds of the initial consonants in words, rather than rhyming, based on the sounds of the controlling vowel in the stem of the final word in a line. Although some of Chaucer's contemporaries still wrote alliterative poetry in the fourteenth century, the rhyming that we find in Chaucer's poetry has dominated much of the poetry after him. By Chaucer's time, in any case, whereas the various Old English inflectional endings had almost disappeared, they were sometimes retained as vestiges in the final -e or "schwa" vowel. I discuss this vowel more fully below, in "Pronunciation and Phonetic Transcription of Chaucer's Middle English," pp. 39–40.

It is interesting to compare three versions of verse 44 of Matthew 13 in the Bible. In the Anglo-Saxon Gospels, written around 1000, we find the passage written thus in Old English:

> **Heofona rice is gelic gehyddum gold-horde on ðam æcere, ðone behyt se man ðe hine fint; and for his blysse gæþ, and sylþ eall ðæt he ah, and gebig ðone æcer.**

That is virtually meaningless to modern readers. To make any sense of the passage we would need to know the basic vocabulary: **heofona** is the genitive case and means "heaven's," **rice** is the nominative case and means "kingdom," **gelic** means "like," **gehyddum** means "hidden," **gold-horde** means "treasure," **æcere** means "field" (etymologically akin to the modern "acre")—and that is only the first third of the verse.

In the Wycliffite Gospels, written around Chaucer's time in Middle English, that same passage is much easier going for us moderns:

> **The kyngdame of heuenes is lijk to tresour hid in a feeld, the which a man that fyndith, hidith; and for ioye of it he goth, and sellith alle thingis that he hath, and bieth the ilk feeld.**

We need to know that **lijk** means "like," **ioye** means "joy," **hath** means "[he] has," **bieth** means "buys," and **ilk** means "same," but beyond those small spelling changes and shifts in vocabulary, the passage is comparatively modern.

It is only a short jump from that Middle English passage to the modern English (though now rather stilted) King James version of 1611:

> **The kingdom of heaven is like unto treasure hid in a field: the which when a man hath found, he hideth, and for joy thereof goeth and selleth all that he hath, and buyeth that field.**

Chaucer's Middle English, like Wycliffe's, is much closer to modern English than it was to Old English.

French loan words

In addition to shifting away from an inflectional grammatical base and an alliterative poetic base, the English of Chaucer's time had vastly enriched its word base by the introduction of many French loan words. Students who have studied modern French have a slightly easier time making their way in Middle English because many of the words will sound familiar. Here are a few of the French loan words introduced by Chaucer's time:

affeccioun	emotion, love
balaunce	balance, scale
charitable	kind, loving
estatliche	dignified, stately
honour	honor

Because of the widespread and permanent influx of French loan words, however, even modern readers who have not studied French have a relatively easy time learning to read and pronounce Middle English because many of the words, like those above, are still with us. While modern English readers cannot without extensive training make much sense of an Old English text, they can, with only a little help from a glossary, a little guidance from a teacher, a little awareness of shifting spelling practices, and a little experience learn to read Chaucerian texts with relative ease. The word list immediately following this chapter is designed to acquaint modern readers with some of the more mystifying meanings of Middle English words.

In Chaucer's time there were several dialects of English. We are fortunate that Chaucer was a Londoner, because the London dialect is the ancestor of most modern varieties of English. Had Chaucer, like the author of *Sir Gawain and the Green Knight*, written in another dialect, we would have a considerably more challenging time with his language. As it is, by keeping a few general pointers in mind, we can with relative ease understand what he wrote. The remainder of this chapter outlines a few of those general pointers.

Personal pronouns

Chaucer used the following forms of the personal pronoun:

SINGULAR PERSONAL PRONOUNS

	First Person	Second Person	Third Person Masculine	Third Person Feminine	Third Person Neuter
Nominative	I	thou	he	she	hit, hyt
Genitive	my, myn	thy, thyn	his	hir, her	his
Indirect Object	me	thee	him	hir, her	him
Direct Object	me	thee	him	hir, her	hit, hyt

PLURAL PERSONAL PRONOUNS

	First Person	Second Person	Third Person
Nominative	we	ye	they
Genitive	oure	youre	hir, her
Indirect Object	us	yow, you	hem
Direct Object	us	yow, you	hem

The **her**, **hir** forms, meaning "her" or "their," occasionally had the letter -e at the end: **here**, **hire**. Note two particular features of pronouns. First, "them" had not yet by Chaucer's time come into the language. Instead Chaucer used **hem**. Second, because the neuter pronoun "its" had not yet entered the language, Chaucer used what is now the masculine pronoun **his**. In the opening lines of the General Prologue, then, **Whan that Aprill with his shoures soote**, the **his** is more properly translated "its" than "his."

Demonstrative pronouns

The demonstrative pronouns were similar enough to modern English forms, **this**, **that**, **these**, but instead of "those" Chaucer wrote **tho**. Be careful, though, because **tho** can also mean "then."

Verb forms

Most verb forms are recognized easily enough. Some verbs have dropped out of modern usage, like **witen**, meaning "to know," but textual glosses will usually identify the meanings. Some verb forms have unusual spellings, like **dorste**, the past tense of "dare." As in modern English, some verbs change their forms by changing a vowel in the stem of the word (e.g., the verb "to bear": **bere**, **bar**), while some keep the stem vowel the same but alter the ending (e.g., the verb "to love": **love**, **loved**). The past participle of many verbs is indicated by a prefix **y-** (occasionally **i-**). This form is a vestige of the Old English prefix **ge-**, which served the same purpose. When the women of Thebes in the *Knight's Tale* see Theseus, they complain that cruel Creon will not let them bury their dead husbands:

> "He, for despit and for his tirannye,
> To do the dede bodyes vileynye
> Of alle oure lordes whiche that been yslawe,

> Hath alle the bodyes on an heep ydrawe,
> And wol nat suffren hem, by noon assent,
> Neither to been yburyed nor ybrent."
> (I 941–46)

The words "slain," "drawn," "buried," and "burned" are all past participles indicated as such by the prefix **y-**. The prefix was pronounced "ee."

Adverbs and "-lich" forms

Most adverbs are easily understood as such by modern readers, but one unusual form for the adverb ends in **-lich** where we might expect an -ly. Thus, **freendlich** would take the place of the modern "friendly." The **-lich** would have been pronounced just as it would be pronounced in modern English, "-litch."

Double negatives and other small differences

There are lots of small differences between modern English and Middle English. One of them, for example, was the use of **myself** as the subject of a sentence, as when the Wife of Bath says, **Myself have been the whippe** (III 175), meaning "I have been the whip." Another is the omission of the subject pronoun where we would have one. Instead of "It befell that one day in that season," Chaucer wrote **Bifil that in that seson on a day** (I 19). He sometimes leaves out other words we might expect, as when he tells us that Dorigen in the *Franklin's Tale* was **the faireste under sonne** (V 754) rather than the **the faireste under the sonne**. You will notice that Chaucer sometimes offers contractions we are not used to. He tells us, for example, that the Knight had a yeoman **and servantz namo** (I 101). Perhaps because he needed a rhyme for **so** in the next line, he wrote **namo** rather than **no more**. The absence of the apostrophe meant that Chaucer had a different way of showing possession. Instead of writing "the carpenter's house" or "the carpenter's wall," he wrote **the carpenteres hous** and **the carpenteris wal** (I 3356, 3359; for the inconsistent spelling of the possessive form of "carpenter's" see the next section). For most such differences, the context makes the meaning clear enough.

Modern readers should be aware especially, however, that our modern rule about double negatives cancelling one another did not apply in Chaucer's time. For Chaucer, a sentence like "I don't have no money" did not mean "I DO have SOME money." Rather, the double—and even triple or quadruple negatives— usually merely intensified the negative: "I REALLY don't have ANY money at ALL." When Chaucer tells us of the Knight that **He nevere yet no vileynye ne sayd** (I 70), the meaning is not that he really did speak villainously, but rather that he TRULY never did. Although Chaucer sometimes used irony to suggest a meaning opposite to what the words say, that irony is less a matter of grammar than of interpretation. When Chaucer tells us of the Sergeant of Law that **Nowher so bisy a man as he ther nas**, the fact that the Sergeant is not really so busy is clear not from the doubling of negatives but from the next line, **And yet he semed bisier than he was** (I 321–22).

Inconsistent spelling

The notion that there was only one "correct" way to spell a given word was not to come until many centuries after Chaucer. Chaucer had multiple spellings for many words, sometimes spelling them rather differently even in lines that appeared close together. Inconsistent spelling simply did not bother either him or the scribes who copied his work. To read Chaucer's words, then, requires a willingness to suffer variety in spelling. One of the features of Chaucer's spelling is that he used the letters **i** and **y** almost interchangeably. **Availle** is sometimes spelled **avaylle**, and **hidous** ("hideous") is sometimes spelled **hydous**. If at first a word with an **i** or a **y** in it appears unfamiliar, try substituting the other letter. There was no difference in pronunciation between the **i** and the **y**. Chaucer sometimes used the single **a** where he other times used the double **aa**. Thus, the modern word "solace," which meant in Chaucer's time "entertainment" (or sometimes "relief" or "refreshment"), might be variously spelled **solas**, or **solaas**, with no change in pronunciation. Chaucer's use of the final -e at the end of a word was somewhat inconsistent. Sometimes he used it, sometimes not. Thus, our adjective "bright" might have been written by Chaucer in at least four ways: **bright**, **bryght**, **brighte**, or **bryghte**. The latter two spellings might indicate that the word is an adverb, "brightly," but it need not mean that. The context is almost always a good guide. The final -e might or might not have been pronounced, depending on its position in a line of poetry. For more on the pronunciation of the final -e, see the sections on the "schwa" and on iambic pentameter in "Pronunciation and Phonetic Transcription of Chaucer's Middle English," pp. 39–41 below.

Word List

Most of the words listed below have meanings that may surprise you. I included them for one of three reasons: 1) they appear with some regularity in Chaucer and so cause students to look them up again and again; 2) they are totally unfamiliar to speakers of modern English and so will thwart the best efforts of guessers; or 3) they look deceptively similar to certain modern English words and so cause students to guess the wrong meanings. It will save you time, confusion, and frustration if you immediately familiarize yourself really thoroughly with the list—even memorize it.

    As you do so, however, pause to enjoy the small lessons in the history of the English language that lie before you. Notice, for example, that our word "ask" derives from the Middle English **axen**, a pronunciation now considered in some circles to be substandard: "I want to ax you a question." It was not substandard for Chaucer. Notice that our word "bald" comes from the Middle English **balled**, or "like a ball"—a vivid description for a man like me with a shiny pate. Notice that the Middle English **verray** meant "true" or "genuine." It was not the general intensifier "very" it became later. Thus, when Chaucer describes the Knight as "a verray, parfit gentil knyght" (I 72), he meant to describe him not as a **verray parfit gentil knyght** or even as "a truly perfect gentle knight," but as "a true and perfect gentle knight." And pause to imagine how the Middle English word **buxom**, meaning "obedient," came to take on its modern meaning describing a female body type, how Middle English **daungerous**, meaning "haughty," may have come to mean "perilous" to us moderns, and how the Middle English **starf**, meaning "to die," came to mean, much more specifically, "to die of hunger."

As you learn the list, you will want to pay particular attention to words that look familiar to us but that have changed meanings, such as: **aventure, coy, disese, drenche, forward, hem, noon, prime, sentence, skille, wood**, and so on. I have given the most common meanings of the words. Keep in mind that in context they may take on different shades of meaning.

alday	continually
alderbest	best of all
algate(s)	at any rate
anon	at once, soon
aton	"at one," together
atones	at once, immediately
atte	at the
aventure	chance
avisen	ponder, consider
axen	ask
balled	bald
benedicite	Lord bless you
bihote	promise
blyve	quickly, soon
brenne	burn
buxom	obedient
cas	chance, accident
certes	certainly

Word list

cherl, carl	lowborn ruffian
clepe	call, name
conne	be able
corage	heart
coy	quiet
daungerous	haughty
disese	discomfort
doom	judgment, opinion
drenche	drown
duren	to last, endure
eek	also
eft	again
elles	else, otherwise
em	uncle
everich	each, every one
fere	companion
ferre	farther
forward	agreement, promise
for-why	because
fowel	bird
fre	generous
gan	began
gentillesse	nobility
gramercy	thank you, "god grant you mercy"
gyse	custom
hem	them
hals	neck
her, hir(e)	their, her
hert	hart, deer
hight	named, promised
him thoughte	it seemed to him
honest	respectable, virtuous, chaste

ilke	like, same
jape	joke, trick
kan	know, know how
kowthe	known
kynde	nature
lemman	lover
lette	hinder, prevent
leve	dear, beloved
levere	prefer, rather
listes	tournament grounds
luste	pleasure, desire
maugre	in spite of
mete	(n.) meal, eating
mete	(adj.) fitting
mete	(vb.) dream
mo	more, others
moot	must, may
mowe	may
namo, namore	no more
nas (ne was)	was not
natheles	nonetheless
neer	near, nearer
nere (ne were)	were not
no fors	no matter
noon	none, no one
not, noot (ne wot)	knows not
nyce	foolish
nys	is not
nys (ne wiste)	did not know
o	one
or	or, before

Word list

paraunter	perhaps, peradventure
parde	by God
pleyn	(adj.) full, complete
pleyne	(vb.) complain
prime	9 AM
pryvee	(adj.) secret(ly)
pryvee	(n.) toilet, privy
quite	repay, requite
rakel	rash, hasty
rathe	early, soon
rede	(vb.) advise, counsel
rede	(n.) advice
save	except
sentence	insight, moral truth
siker(ly)	sure(ly)
sithen	since
skille	reason
skilful	discerning
solas	entertainment
starf	die
stinte	stop, interrupt
swevene	dream
swich	such
swive	make love to
swynk	work
ther	where
thilke	the same, that
tho	(adv.) then
tho	(pron.) those
trouthe	honesty, promise
trowe	believe, think

unnethe	scarcely
verray	true, genuine
wend	think, suppose
wende	go, wander
whilom	once, formerly
wight	man, person
wiste	knew
withhouten drede	without doubt
wone	custom
wood	(adj.) mad, insane
worship	honor
wot	know
wyde	spacious
ye	you
ye, yen	eye, eyes
yeman	yeoman, attendant
yerne	eagerly
yfeere	together
yif	if
ywis	certainly

Pronunciation and Phonetic Transcription of Chaucer's Middle English

Chaucer's poetry sounds quite beautiful when it is spoken by someone who has learned how to pronounce it as Chaucer himself might have. How do we know how he would have spoken his words, said his lines? Although several generations of scholars have worked on just those questions, none would say that we do know precisely how Chaucer would have spoken his own poetry. There is now general agreement, however, on the main principles of the pronunciation of his Middle English. Others have learned those principles. You can, too, especially if you read and then carefully reread this chapter and have the help of an encouraging teacher. You may also want to listen to some of the recordings of the Chaucer Studio at Brigham Young University (http://creativeworks.byu.edu/chaucer) or avail yourself of the technical devices of METRO (Middle English Teaching Resources Online) at Harvard (http://metro.fas.harvard.edu). But above all, remember the three p-words persistence, practice, and Poppins. Why Poppins? Well, you surely remember Mary Poppins's famous song, "Supercalifragilisticexpialidocious"? Your pronunciation of Middle English will be a bit like that. Even though the sound of it at first seems quite atrocious, if you chew this chapter like a terrier ferocious, your friends will listen to you speak and say you are precocious!

Phonetic alphabet

Learning and recording the sounds of Chaucer's poetry is more convenient with a phonetic alphabet, each symbol of which represents one sound—as opposed to our regular alphabet, each letter of which might represent several sounds. Our letter *a*, for example, represents different sounds in each of the following four modern English words: *father, fathom, fame, fawn*. In the phonetic alphabet, on the other hand, there are distinct symbols for the vowel sounds of each of these words: [ɑ], [æ], [e], [ɔ], respectively. Each of these symbols represents one sound and one sound only, and so can be used unambiguously to indicate a specific sound.

It is important to note that phonetic symbols represent sounds, not letters. That is, the number of phonetic symbols used to indicate the sound of a word may be greater or (more frequently) smaller than the number of letters used to spell the word in our regular alphabet. Thus our modern word *knight* becomes, phonetically, simply [nɑɪt], because the *k* and the *gh* no longer indicate pronounced sounds. In Chaucer's time, however, the **k** and the **gh** were pronounced, so a phonetic transcription of Chaucer's word **knyght** would be more complicated: [knɪxt]. There is no phonetic distinction between upper- and lower-case letters. Thus, the symbol for the consonant cluster at the start of **Chaucer** and **child** is the same: [tʃ].

Obviously, then, one of our first tasks is to become familiar with a phonetic alphabet. Several of these have been developed over the years. The one presented here is based on the International Phonetic Alphabet (IPA). Note that phonetic symbols are set off within square brackets to distinguish them from ordinary letters.

Consonants

Most **boldfaced** letters and words in these pages are **Middle English** words; most non-bold *italicized* words are in *modern English*; the bracketed symbols are [fonɛtɪk sɪmbɛlz].

Consonants

You will have no great difficulty with Chaucer's consonants because they are usually pronounced the same as our modern English consonants. Nor will you have great difficulty with the phonetic transcription of consonants, for the IPA symbols often look the same as letters in our regular alphabet. Only a few of the symbols in Chart 1 (see page 30) will be new to you.

The first two columns in Chart 1 show (1) the spelling in Middle English that ordinarily yields the sound represented by the IPA symbol, and (2) an example of the letter in a Middle English word. The last two columns show (3) the IPA symbol for the sound, in brackets, and (4) a modern English word, the underlined letters of which indicate the sound assigned to the symbol.

As the chart indicates, modern English pronunciation is a fairly reliable guide to Middle English pronunciation of consonants. Take note, however, of the trilled **r**, of the guttural **gh**, and of the two sounds possible for **s** and **th** spellings.

(1) The **s** in Chaucer's words was voiced [z] when it came between two vowels, as in **esed**, but voiceless [s] when not intervocalic, as in **is, est, inspired**, and **sonne**. "Voiced" consonants are those for which the vocal chords vibrate. Try lightly gripping your thumb and forefinger just above your Adam's apple, with one on either side, and say aloud the word *hiss*. You will not feel your vocal chords vibrate. That s-sound [s] is said to be "voiceless" because you make the sound with your tongue and your teeth, without using your voice. Now, without removing your thumb and forefinger, say the word *his*. You will feel the vocal chords vibrating, indicating that you are

voicing the sound [z]. Now, keeping your thumb and forefinger in place, slowly say "His hiss was loud." If you don't feel the difference in vocal vibration in your fingers, say the sentence louder.

Plurals, such as Middle English **houses**, and other words ending in s would have ended with the voiceless [s], though this would have been voiced [z] before a word beginning with a vowel. So, **as I lay** is transcribed [ɑz i læɪ]. The double ss, as in **gentilesse**, was voiceless, even when intervocalic. An initial s following a word ending in a vowel would still be [s], though: **the chambres and the stables** is transcribed [θɛ tʃɑmbrɛz ɑnd θɛ stɑblɛs].

(2) The **th** in Chaucer's words was voiced [ð] between vowels, as in **oother**, but voiceless [θ] when not intervocalic, as in **thynk**. Note that modern English practice is often similar, as in *other* (voiced) and *think* (voiceless). The th is usually voiceless, even at the end of a word that precedes a word starting with a vowel. So, **inspired hath in** is transcribed [ɪnspirɛd hɑθ ɪn].

Note also that in certain positions, consonants that have become silent in modern English would have been given a distinct pronunciation in Chaucer's time:

(3) **k** and **g** before **n**, in words like **knyght, knowe, gnawe**, would have been distinctly pronounced, as they still are in our words *acknowledge* and *recognize*. However, gn in French loan-words had the sound [n]: **digne, signes**, etc.

(4) l before d, f, v, k, m, in words like **wold, calf, halve, folk, palmer**, would have been pronounced.

(5) **w** before **r** initially, as in **write, wrecche**, was pronounced. Remember to trill the r here and elsewhere in Chaucer.

(6) **h** after initial **w**, as in **whyle, which**, would have been pronounced first with a distinct expiration of breath as in our exclamation *whew!* Thus, [hwilə], [hwɪtʃ].

Consonants

(7) **g** after **n** in stressed syllables, as in **thyng**, **singer**, would have been pronounced, as in modern English *finger*; thus, [θɪŋg], [sɪŋgɛr]. In unstressed positions, such as the final **-yng**, **-ing**, of present participles, the **ng** combination would have been given the simple nasal pronunciation [ŋ] it still has today. The **nk** spelling would ordinarily have been pronounced [ŋk], as it still is in modern English *think*.

(8) Double consonants are transcribed only once; thus **alle** is [ɑlə], **atte**, is [ɑtə], etc.

CHART 1: CONSONANTS

Middle English Spelling	Middle English Example	Middle English Pronunciation	Pronounced like underlined letter(s) in modern English word:
b	bachelor	[b]	boy
c, k	cart (c before a, o, u)	[k]	cat
c	certeyn (c before i, e)	[s]	city
ch	chivalrie	[tʃ]	church
d	daunce	[d]	dog
f	fleen	[f]	fear
g	gape (before a, o, u)	[g]	gate
g	gentil (before i, e)	[dʒ]	gentle
gh	knyght	[x]	Ger. ich, nach)
h	haste	[h]	hair (or silent)
j	jugge	[dʒ]	judge
l	lak	[l]	less
m	manere	[m]	mud
n	noble	[n]	nothing
ng	lovyng (unaccented)	[ŋ]	sing
ng	yong (accented)	[ŋg]	finger
p	pitee	[p]	pant
q	quite	[k]	quest
r	reve	[r]	royal
s	sapience	[s]	sock
s, z	resoun	[z]	zest
sh	shadwe	[ʃ]	share
t	tretee	[t]	trouble
th	thonder	[θ]	thin
th	bathe	[ð]	then
v	verray	[v]	vast
w	wydwe	[w]	west
x	axeth	[ks]	ox
y	yong	[j]	young

Vowels and diphthongs

Chaucer's vowels and diphthongs (vowel glides, or sounds made by gliding two more or less distinct vowel sounds together) are more difficult for us to learn to pronounce than his consonants. To be sure, many of the "short" vowels (such as e in **bed**, i in **skille**, and u in **ful**) are pronounced as they still are today. A great many of Chaucer's vowels, however, have shifted in sound quality down through the years. No one fully understands why these shifts took place, but we do know that, gradually between 1400 and 1600, shift they did. The phenomenon is now called the "Great Vowel Shift." Before it was identified, students assumed that Chaucer was a poor and inconsistent rhymster. Now we know that almost always his rhymes are true; we were merely reading his vowels as we would pronounce them today, not as he would have pronounced them in the late 1300s.

The most efficient way for modern students to learn to pronounce Chaucer's vowels as he would have pronounced them is to try to "reverse" the Great Vowel Shift. We know in what ways Chaucer's vowels shifted during that transition period. What we must do, then, when we see a Chaucerian word, is to leap mentally ahead and think how the word is spelled and pronounced now, then leap back, applying in reverse the "rule" that governed the shift. The task may seem impossibly plodding and slow-moving at first, but if you apply yourself diligently your halting stumbles will become graceful bounds. You will be rewarded by the sound of your own voice tripping mellifluously along in Middle English.

Chart 2 represents an attempt to simplify the most important vowel rules you will have to know to get along respectably at Middle English pronunciation. No chart of this kind can cover all situations. There were exceptions to the rules even in Chaucer's time, if only because English in his time was already a mongrel language, the bastard offspring of several generations of irresponsible bedfellows.

The situation is complicated further because some Chaucerian words have dropped out of common usage or been altered so much that the chart cannot help you much. Chaucerian **soote**, for example, means *sweet*, not *sooty*, and Chaucerian **parfit** becomes modern *perfect*. Such words reflect changes in word meaning and spelling that will render difficult or uncertain your use of the chart, for the chart is based on the assumption that vowels and word meanings have not changed.

A related difficulty is that your use of the chart will be somewhat limited at first by your limited vocabulary. How would you pronounce the Middle English word **bryd**, for example? Since the chart conversions are based on the current spelling and pronunciation of words, you would need to know whether Chaucer's word means *bride*, *bread*, *bird*, *broad*, or *breed*. Now, of course, you must examine the context carefully to determine the meaning or else consult a Middle English dictionary. A Chaucer glossary will serve you just as well for this purpose, however, and a glossary, included in most modern editions of Chaucer's works, should tell you that **bryd** means *bird*. Since the *i* in *bird* is "short," you would know (from the chart) that it was short in Chaucer's word also, and so you would know that the vowel must be pronounced [ɪ]. If you had guessed *bride* as the meaning of **bryd**, you would have had not only the wrong meaning, but also the wrong pronunciation for the Middle English word.

Vowels and dipththongs

CHART 2: VOWELS AND DIPHTHONGS

Middle English Spelling	Middle English Example	Middle English Pronunciation	Pronounced like underlined letter(s) in modern English word:
a, aa	that, bathed	[ɑ]	f<u>a</u>ther—pronounced this way always, even though the vowel quality for the <u>a</u> is variously pronounced in modern English.
ai, ay **ei, ey**	lai, day feith, veyne	[æɪ]	<u>ai</u>sle—pronounced this way always. Because [æɪ] is a diphthong, emphasize the glide from [æ] to [ɪ], almost as if it were two syllables. Middle English **day**, then, sounded more like modern English *die* than modern English *day*, and Middle English **veyne** sounded more like our *vine* than our *vein*.
au, aw	faught, lawe	[ɑʊ]	h<u>ou</u>se, s<u>au</u>erkr<u>au</u>t—pronounced this way always.

CHART 2: VOWELS AND DIPHTHONGS, continued

Middle English Spelling	Middle English Example	Middle English Pronunciation	Pronounced like underlined letter(s) in modern English word:
e, ee	gentil, end	[ε]	b<u>e</u>d, fr<u>ie</u>nd—pronounced this way when the word in question has a "short" vowel today—as in *bed, better, end* [ε].
e, ee	fredom	[e]	f<u>a</u>te, s<u>a</u>ke—pronounced this way when the word in question has a "long" vowel today—as in *seek* [i]—and when it is not spelled *ea* today.
e, ee	heeth	[æ]	<u>a</u>t, s<u>a</u>lmon—pronounced this way when the word in question has a "long" vowel today—as in *season* [i] or *great* [e]—and when it is spelled with an *ea* today.
e	pilgrymage	[ə]	sof<u>a</u>, <u>a</u>bove—pronounced this way at the end of certain words. See the special note on "schwa" below, pp. 39–40.
e	clerk	[ɑ]	b<u>ar</u>n, d<u>ar</u>k—See Free tip 3, p. 43.

CHART 2: VOWELS AND DIPHTHONGS, continued

Middle English Spelling	Middle English Example	Middle English Pronunciation	Pronounced like underlined letter(s) in modern English word:
eau, ew	fewe, lewed, dew, shewe, shrewe, beaute, hewe	[ευ]	Not duplicated in modern English; sounds like "<u>eh</u>-oo"—pronounced this way only in the words listed and in a few more infrequently used words.
eu, ew	newl, reule	[ɪu]	f<u>ew</u>, m<u>ew</u>—pronounced this way usually, except for the words listed in the previous item.
i, y	skille	[ɪ]	b<u>i</u>t, l<u>i</u>d—pronounced this way when the word in question has a "short" vowel today—as in *with* [ɪ], *liquor* [ɪ].
i, y	ryde	[i]	f<u>ee</u>t, m<u>e</u>ter—pronounced this way when the word in question has a "long" vowel or dipthong (vowel glide) today—as in the final vowel in *melody* [i] or the *i* in *white* [ɑɪ].

Note: The letter **y** is usually a vowel, but can sometimes act as a consonant, as in **yong** (*young*) and **yate** (*gate*). In past participles where the y precedes the verb stem (**ytaught, yronne**) transcribe and pronounce it [i].

CHART 2: VOWELS AND DIPHTHONGS, continued

Middle English Spelling	Middle English Example	Middle English Pronunciation	Pronounced like underlined letter(s) in modern English word:
oi, oy	coy, boidekyn	[ɔɪ]	c<u>oy</u>, b<u>oy</u>—pronounced this way always.
o, oo	ofte, hooly	[ɔ]	d<u>o</u>g, <u>ough</u>t—pronounced this way when the word in question has a "short" vowel today—as in *hot* [a], *would* [ʊ], *thong* [ɔ]—or a "long" vowel as in *most* and *stone* [o].
o, oo	love	[ʊ]	b<u>u</u>ll, b<u>oo</u>k—pronounded this way when the word in question has the [ʌ] sound today—as in *duck, monk, nun*.
o, oo	roote	[o]	n<u>o</u>te, l<u>ow</u>—pronounced this way when the word in question has come into modern English pronounced [u]—as in *food*—or when the word is spelled with <u>oo</u> today even if the vowel is "short" today, as in *good* [ʊ], and *blood* [ʌ].

Vowels and diphthongs

CHART 2: VOWELS AND DIPHTHONGS, continued

Middle English Spelling	Middle English Example	Middle English Pronunciation	Pronounced like underlined letter(s) in modern English word:
ou, ow	fowles, flour	[u]	<u>oo</u>ze, sh<u>oe</u>—pronounced this way usually, except when the word in question is pronounced [o] today (see next item).
ou, ow	knowen, soule	[ɔu]	cr<u>aw</u>l, P<u>au</u>l, (pronounced as if disyllabic)—pronounced this way when the word in question has come into modern English pronounced [o]—as in *know, soul*.
u	ful, lusty	[ʊ]	f<u>u</u>ll, b<u>oo</u>k—pronounced this way always.

Note: **ow** is almost always to be taken as a single vowel and transcribed either [u] or, more rarely, [ɔu]. Occasionally in compound words the letters are to be separated. Thus, for the word **toward**, a combination of **to** and **ward**, separate the **o** from the **w**: [towɑrd] rather than [tuɑrd].

Be especially precise in transcribing vowels:

[ɑ] is **not** the same as [æ];
[e] is **not** the same as [ɛ];
[ɪ] is **not** the same as [i];
[ʊ] is **not** the same as [u].

More on vowels

Chart 3 is designed to give you a quick summary of the modern English sound equivalents of the phonetic symbols for vowels. The left column gives the vowel symbol, the right column gives a modern English word that has that vowel sound. This chart is not a summary of the transcription rules but, rather, a summary of the sounds of the IPA vowel and diphthong symbols.

CHART 3: SOUNDS OF PHONETIC SYMBOLS FOR VOWELS

IPA symbol for vowel or diphthong	Sound in a modern English word
[ɑ]	f<u>a</u>ther
[æ]	h<u>a</u>t
[ɑɪ]	m<u>y</u>
[æɪ]	<u>ai</u>sle
[ɑʊ]	h<u>ou</u>se
[ɛ]	b<u>e</u>d
[e]	f<u>a</u>te
[ɛʊ]	"eh-oo"
[ə]	<u>a</u>bove
[ɪ]	b<u>i</u>t
[i]	f<u>ee</u>t
[ɪʊ]	f<u>ew</u>
[o]	kn<u>ow</u>
[ʊ]	b<u>u</u>ll
[u]	b<u>oo</u>t
[ʌ]	m<u>o</u>nk
[ɔ]	<u>ou</u>ght
[ɔɪ]	b<u>oy</u>
[ɔʊ]	cr<u>awl</u>

Little words

It is a good idea to memorize the sounds of the personal pronouns and certain little words so that they become automatic. For example, **I**, the first personal pronoun, was pronounced [i], or "ee." **He**, **she**, **we**, and **me** all had the vowel sound [e] in Middle English, or "hay," "shay," "way," and "may." **To** had the [o] sound, "toe"; **so** had the [ɔ] sound, "saw." All those words with the solo vowel **a**, **aa** had the sound [ɑ], so **al**, **that**, and the article **a** all rhymed with the first syllable in modern *father*. But not all the little words have changed sounds. **It** had the same vowel sound [ɪ] it still has, "it." And **you**, even when spelled **yow**, had the same vowel sound [u] it still has today, "you."

The "schwa"

The unstressed **e** at the end of many Middle English words is sometimes known as the "schwa" vowel. It is written phonetically [ə] and pronounced like the rather nondescript unaccented first syllable of modern English *above* [əbʌv]. This weak-hearted "uh" sound is found at the end of a great many words in Middle English, and could be pronounced as a separate syllable: **roote** [rotə], **swete** [swetə], **wende** [wendə]. By Chaucer's time the terminal -e had apparently ceased to be pronounced by most people in ordinary speech, but Chaucer nevertheless appears to have expected those who read his poetry to continue a poetic convention by pronouncing it in certain situations: "roat-uh," "swayt-uh," "wend-uh."

The terminal -e is pronounced (1) when it appears at the end of a line of poetry, unless it is the only vowel in the word (e.g., **me**, **be**), and (2) occasionally when the iambic meter requires it at the end of a word that appears inside the line (see section on iambic pentameter, pp. 40–42 below).

The "schwa" symbol [ə] indicates technically the same sound as [ʌ], but is used only for the unaccented -e at the end of certain words. The symbol [ʌ] is used in transcribing modern English words. It is not used in transcribing Middle English words because that sound does not appear in Middle English except in unaccented positions, where the symbol [ə] is more appropriate.

If the metrical configuration of the line permits it, the final -e in a word is elided (that is, slurred or blended) before a word beginning with a vowel.

Other unstressed e's

In some multisyllabic words an internal **e** can be dropped or slurred to remove an "extra" syllable, if the meter of the line requires it. Such e's are usually transcribed [ɛ] unless they are dropped. For example, the first e in **chapeleyne** [tʃɑpɛlæɪnə] or the middle e in **felaweshipe** [fɛlɑuɛʃɪpə], and **hevenes** [hɛvɛnɛs] can be dropped if these words appear in positions where the iambic rhythm of the line suggests that a syllable can best be dropped.

Iambic pentameter

Much of Chaucer's poetry is written in what are called iambic pentameter rhymed couplets. An "iambic foot" is a metrical unit consisting of an unaccented syllable (indicated by a "ᴜ" over the syllable) followed by an accented syllable (indicated by an accent mark "/" over the syllable):

    ᴜ /   ᴜ /
    about   concern

Iambic pentameter 41

"Pentameter" refers to five such iambic feet in the same line, as in:

ᴗ   /   ᴗ   /   ᴗ   /   ᴗ   /   ᴗ   /
And bathed every veyne in swich licour.

In the lines ending in a "schwa" [ə] there is an extra unaccented syllable (an eleventh syllable) after the last iambic foot, as in:

ᴗ   /   ᴗ   /   ᴗ   /   ᴗ   /   ᴗ   /   ᴗ
The droghte of March hath perced to the roote.

A "rhymed couplet" is a pair of lines the last two words of which rhyme. You will occasionally have to experiment a little with a line in an effort to get the line to "scan" or read smoothly. But do not try too hard. Do not make the lines sound too much like regular "jog-trot." Some lines are simply short a syllable, and Chaucer seems not to have tried for perfect regularity in scansion.

To understand how to read iambic pentameter in Middle English it is useful for you to write some iambic pentameter lines in modern English. To do so it is necessary first to figure out where the natural stress or accent in words is, and then to place those words in a five-stress line so that the first syllable of the line is unaccented. The next and and every second syllable after that is accented. In the modern English "Nicholas was a horny young student" we have the necessary ten syllables, but they are not iambic pentameter. The line can be made to sound iambic only if we change the natural emphasis of the first and last words: "Nicholas **was a horny young** student." Much better would be this line: "This Nicholas, he was a horny stud," because it places the naturally stressed syllables in the second, fourth, sixth, eighth, and last positions in the line: "This **Nicholas, he was a horny stud.**" Here are eight lines of pretty good modern English iambic pentameter:

> The carpenter loved Alison, his wife,
> But he was old and she was full of life.
> When Nicholas came near and begged for love
> She thought that he might fit her like a glove.
> Sweet Alison then played a clever trick.
> She dumped old John so she could jump young Nick.
> This clever lass, she had the wherewithall
> To leap from tub to bed and have a ball.

Part of the trick of writing iambic verse is to start each line with an unaccented word or syllable. "This **Nicholas** . . ." works, because "This" is unaccented. Starting with "**Nicholas** . . ." throws the rest of the line off, because the first syllable of "Nicholas" is accented. Do not end lines with words that have naturally unaccented closing syllables, like "**eat**ing" or "**dish**es." It is usually most effective to put the important words or parts of words in positions in the line that automatically carry an iambic emphasis—that is, the second, fourth, sixth, eighth, and tenth syllables. Go ahead. Try a few modern English rhyming couplets. You can do it. Start by writing second iambic lines to rhyme with these:

> The knight jumped off his horse and ran away.

> I like old Chaucer, but I must confess

> This morning I got up and made my bed.

Free tips

(1) The ending **-ioun** (occasionally spelled **-ion**) was always distinctly disyllabic: **passioun** [pasɪun], **nacioun** [nasɪun]. It was not given the monosyllabic "-shun" sound it has today.

(2) A number of words, particularly French loan-words like the following, were accented differently by Chaucer than they are today: **coráge, corál, manére, monéye, persévere, solémpnely, honóur, viságe**. In addition, certain other words, too numerous to list, might be accented differently at different times, depending on the metrical requirements of the lines in which they occur. Sometimes a little experimenting is necessary to make a line scan smoothly. But don't try too hard. Some lines are, simply, irregular.

(3) The Middle English vowel e followed by r would probably have had its modern British [ɑ] pronunciation in a few words: **berne** (barn), **clerk** (clerk), **derk** (dark), **ers** (arse), **ferre** (far), **ferther** (farther), **herke** (hark), **hert(e)** (hart, heart), **person** (parson), **sterre** (star), **sterte** (start), **weere** (war), **werte** (wart), **yerde** (yard). In words other than these, pronounce it [ɛ].

(4) Be on the lookout for contractions. Chaucer, for example, contracted **at the** to **atte**, and **ne wot** (meaning "don't know") to **not**.

(5) Because he wrote before there were fixed and firm rules about spelling, Chaucer's spelling is usually a good indication of pronunciation. Thus, the Chaucerian **temple** would have been pronounced "tem-pluh," not our modern "tem-pul." And the **gh** was always [x], not the silent indicator it is in modern *sight* or the [f] of modern *enough*.

(6) Keep in mind that the phonetic rules in this book do not represent an exact science. Some words—particularly

Middle English words that do not have a modern English equivalent—will not be covered, so for these words you will have to guess. Keep in mind also that Chaucer would almost certainly have pronounced the same words slightly differently in different contexts and for different emphases. And keep in mind, finally, that different modern Chaucerians would read a passage in Chaucer in somewhat varying ways. These "rules," then, are designed merely to help you to achieve a reasonable approximation of Chaucer's pronunciation.

Practicing Transcription of Chaucer's Middle English

You are ready now to try your hand at transcribing the sounds of some of Chaucer's words and lines. I'll walk you through a line, then give you three exercises so you can do some lines yourself.

Transcribing a line

Before he tells his tale, the Miller says, "**That I am dronke, I knowe it by my soun**" (I 3138). We can tell readily enough that he knows by the sound of his own voice that he is drunk, but how are we to pronounce the line? The answer is easy: just take one letter at a time and apply the rules in the previous chapter.

That   The **th** is not between vowels, so is [θ]. The **a** is always [ɑ], and the **t** is an easy [t]. So: [θɑt].

I   The pronoun is a "long" vowel glide [ɑɪ] today, so in Middle English it would have been pronounced [i].

am   The **a** is an easy [ɑ], the **m** an easy [m]. So: [ɑm].

dronke   The **d** and the **r** are an easy [d] and [r], though of course the latter would be trilled. Because the **o** is pronounced [ʌ] in modern English *drunk*, it was [ʊ] in Middle English. The **nk** was always the nasal [ŋk];

it still is today. The final **e** is not needed to fill out the iambic pentameter in the line.

$$\breve{}\quad/\quad\breve{}\quad/\quad\breve{}\quad/\quad\breve{}\quad/\quad\breve{}\quad/$$
That I am dronke, I knowe it by my soun.

Therefore, it is silent here. So: [**druŋk**].

I Same as above: [i].

knowe The hard **k** before **n** was still pronounced in Chaucer's time, so the **kn** is [kn]. Because the modern English vowel **ow** in *know* is pronounced [o], we conclude that the Middle English sound was the diphthong [ɔʊ]. The meter does not require an extra syllable, so the final **e** is silent: [**knɔʊ**].

it Because the **i** in modern *it* is short [ɪ] we know that it was in Chaucer's time, also. So: [**ɪt**].

by The vowel **y** is a diphthong [ɑi] today, and so was [i] in Chaucer's time. So: [**bi**].

my Same as above. So : [**mi**].

soun The **s** is not between vowels, so would have been pronounced [s]. The **ou** was pronounced [u] unless the word it contains is pronounced [o] today. Modern *sound* is not pronounced [**sond**]. So: [**sun**].

By systematically applying our principles, then, we come up with the proper pronunciation of the line:

[θɑt i ɑm druŋk i knɔʊ ɪt bi mi sun]

Start with the spelling, end with the pronouncing

As you struggle to work out the consonant and vowel sounds of Chaucer's lines, remember to begin with the spelling of the Middle English word. By applying the rules in charts 1 and 2 you will soon see the patterns and, in effect, memorize them. You will learn, for example, that the spelling a or aa in Chaucer is always pronounced [ɑ]. The spelling u is always pronounced [ʊ]. The spelling i is always either [ɪ] (if the word is pronounced [ɪ] today, as in *his*), or [i] (if the word is pronounced [ɑɪ] today, as in *bright*). And so on.

When a vowel appears in combination with another vowel, look first for the combined vowels in chart 2. Thus, in the Middle English word **plough**, look first for the **ou** combination on the vowel chart—thus [u]—not an **o** and then a **u** separately. Similarly, in the first syllable of the Middle English **Caunterbury**, treat the **a** and the **u** not as separate vowels, but as a combined vowel—thus [ɑʊ]. Remember that Chaucer seems to have allowed himself some freedom to adjust the pronunciation of words to their place in an iambic pentameter line. I suspect, for example, that Chaucer would have pronounced the -**bury** part of **Caunterbury** as [bri] in line 22 of the General Prologue but as [bʊri] in line 27.

And don't forget to say aloud the sounds you have transcribed. That's what this process is all about. Putting the phonetic transcription on a page is a means to an end, not an end in itself. Be sure to speak the letters, words, and lines as you transcribe them. Stick with it. It may be be slow going at first, but before long pronouncing Middle English will be nearly automatic for you.

In *An ABC of Reading*, Ezra Pound wrote, "Anyone who is too lazy to master the comparatively small glossary necessary to understand Chaucer deserves to be shut out from the reading of good books forever." So much for vocabulary. As for pronunciation, remember that quitters sin, never win. When in doubt, loudly shout. Be diligent, Millicent. Be steady, Teddy. You *will* learn to pronounce Middle English. Whether you pronounce it sweetly or sootily will depend on how seriously you attempt to learn the material in these pages. When you are done, Chaucer, if he could hear you, might be amused at your funny accent, but he would probably recognize his lines.

Phonetic exercises

To help you learn to use the International Phonetic Alphabet, to give you practice in applying the principles you have been reading about in this booklet, and to move you further toward your goal of pronouncing Chaucer's Middle English, I have devised three exercises.

For each of the exercises I give on the left-side pages (50, 52, 54) my own transcriptions of some of Chaucer's words and lines. I strongly urge you to cover up my transcriptions and try them on your own. When you are done you can compare your transcription with mine. If we differ, try to figure out how I got my transcription, then decide whether you prefer your own. If you are part of a formal class, perhaps your teacher will help you to decide which is the better choice.

Then go on to the exercises on the right-side pages (51, 53, 55). I urge you to make enlarged copies of these three pages so that you will have more space for your transcriptions. Having those separate worksheets will also allow you to have this booklet open to the appropriate consonant and vowel charts as you find the phonetic symbols you are looking for.

Put the transcriptions just above the Middle English word. Use brackets for single words, but when transcribing whole lines you can skip the brackets . Remember to be very precise in forming the phonetic symbols. You must print each one separately. There is no way to work in cursive when using

Phonetic exercises 49

phonetic symbols. I urge you to work in pencil and to have an eraser close by.

If you find that transcribing a certain word frustrates you, recall that not all words can be transcribed with great assurance. If the word has no modern English form or if the spelling has shifted dramatically in the past six centuries, you may not be able to apply the principles of the Great Vowel Shift. In such cases, you'll have to guess. Learning to pronounce Middle English is a science, but not an exact science. Languages, like artists and kangaroos, sometimes refuse to be corralled by rules and principles.

Don't forget to say aloud—at least in a whisper—the words and lines you transcribe. When I taught Chaucer I scheduled individual appointments with my students in the third or fourth week of the semester. I had them read some Chaucer aloud to me. I also had them recite six or eight lines they had memorized describing one of the pilgrims Chaucer met at the Tabard Inn. Part of the game was that I had to try to identify the pilgrim being described. I sometimes made a mistake. When I misidentified one of them, it was because I confused the Monk and the Friar, say, or the Squire and the Yeoman. The students almost always, applying the principles in this booklet, said the words and lines just fine.

You can, too.

[gʊd lʌk — ænd hæv fʌn.]

Phonetic exercise 1

Instructions: Transcribe each of the following words into the phonetic alphabet. Because the sounds of many Middle English vowels can be determined by their sounds in modern English, first write down the phonetic sound of the word in modern English and then, applying the rules on the previous pages, write down the sound of the word as it would have been pronounced in Middle English. The first seven have been done for you as examples. You should cover these transcriptions and try your own, then compare your transcription with the printed one to see if you are getting the hang of it. After completing this page, do the next page. For the Middle English, transcribe each final e with the "schwa" symbol [ə], though of course within an actual line of poetry it might not have been pronounced. In the final couplet (lines I 35–36), transcribe the words as they would have been pronounced within those lines.

Modern English	Middle English
[nem] name	[nɑmə] name
[waɪd] wide	[widə] wyde
[θʌm] thumb	[θumbə] thombe
[sɛnd] send	[sɛndə] sende
[slip] sleep	[slepə] sleepe
[bist] beast	[bæst] beest
[tu] to	[to] to

Phonetic exercise 1

Modern English	Middle English
also	also
son	sone
plow	plough
cause	cause
few	fewe
low	lowe
ran	yronne
joy	joye
wheat	whete
without	withoute
showers	shoures
crow	crowe

But nathelees, whil I have tyme and space,

Er that I ferther in this tale pace.

Phonetic exercise 2

Instructions: The following passage is from the General Prologue, lines 19–34. The first six lines have been transcribed for you. Cover these transcriptions when you do your own transcription of these six lines, then compare the two transcriptions. Then finish transcribing the passage on the following page. Remember that the lines are in iambic pentameter, as that will affect your transcription of unaccented **e**'s. For this exercise you may omit brackets.

bifıl	θat	ın	θat	sæzʊn	ɔn	ɑ	daɪ
Bifil	that	in	that	seson	on	a	day,

ın	suθwɛrk	at	θɛ	tɑbɑrd	ɑz	i	laɪ
In	Southwerk	at	the	Tabard	as	I	lay

rɛdi	to	wɛndɛn	ɔn	mi	pılgrımɑdʒə
Redy	to	wenden	on	my	pilgrymage

to	kɑʊntɛrbri	wıθ	fʊl	devʊt	kɔrɑdʒə
To	Caunterbury	with	ful	devout	corage,

at	nixt	was	kʊm	ınto	θat	hɔstɛlriə
At	nyght	was	come	into	that	hostelrye

wɛl	nin	ɑnd	twɛnti	ın	ɑ	kʊmpæıniə
Wel	nyne	and	twenty	in	a	compaignye,

Phonetic exercise 2

Of sondry folk, by aventure yfalle

In felaweshipe, and pilgrimes were they alle,

That toward Caunterbury wolden ryde.

The chambres and the stables weren wyde,

And wel we weren esed atte beste.

And shortly, whan the sonne was to reste,

So hadde I spoken with hem everichon

That I was of hir felaweshipe anon,

And made forward erly for to ryse,

To take oure wey ther as I yow devyse.

Phonetic exercise 3

Instructions: The following passage is from the *Knight's Tale*, lines 1251–67. It should be pretty easy for you to transcribe it, now that you are an expert. Again, the first six lines are done for you, so cover the transcriptions until you have done your own, then compare. Do notice, though, that I have dropped the transcription of the final -e in the word **mordre** because I think it would have been elided with the following word **or** to accommodate the iambic pentameter. When you are done, read the whole passage aloud and be ready to discuss the implications of Arcite's deathbed summary of the human condition.

ɑlɑs	hwi	plæinɛn	fɔlk	sɔ	ɪn	kɔmunə
Allas,	why	pleynen	folk	so	in	commune

ɔn	purvæiɑuns	uf	gɔd	ɔr	uf	fɔrtunə
On	purveiaunce	of	God,	or	of	Fortune,

θɑt	jɛvɛθ	hɛm	ful	ɔft	ɪn	mɑni	ɑ	gizə
That	yeveth	hem	ful	ofte	in	many	a	gyse

wɛl	bɛtrɛ	θɑn	θæi	kɑn	hɛmsɛlf	devizə
Wel	bettre	than	they	kan	hemself	devyse?

sʊm	mɑn	desirɛθ	fɔr	to	hɑn	rɪtʃɛsə
Som	man	desireth	for	to	han	richesse,

θɑt	kɑuz	ɪz	uf	hɪs	mɔrdr	ɔr	græt	sɪknɛsə
That	cause	is	of	his	mordre	or	greet	siknesse;

Phonetic exercise 3

And som man wolde out of his prisoun fayn,

That in his hous is of his meynee slayn.

Infinite harmes been in this mateere.

We witen nat what thing we preyen heere:

We faren as he that dronke is as a mous.

A dronke man woot wel he hath an hous,

But he noot which the righte wey is thider,

And to a dronke man the wey is slider.

And certes, in this world so faren we;

We seken faste after felicitee,

But we goon wrong ful often, trewely.

Printed in Great Britain
by Amazon